Original title:
True Calling

Author: Clement Portlander

ISBN HARDBACK: 978-9916-88-036-4
ISBN PAPERBACK: 978-9916-88-037-1

The Unseen Thread

In shadows deep, a whisper flows,
A bond unseen, where silence grows.
With every breath, the heart does know,
The ties that bind, though none can show.

Through tangled paths, we weave and wend,
Connecting souls that time won't end.
A gentle pull, a silent call,
In unseen threads, we rise, we fall.

In Search of Resonance

With every beat, the echoes ring,
In quiet spaces, hope takes wing.
In search of hearts that understand,
We walk the world, hand in hand.

The chords of life, they intertwine,
Creating music, pure and fine.
In whispered dreams, we find our way,
A symphony of souls in play.

Unbroken Journey

Through winding roads, the stories flow,
Each step we take, the wiser grow.
With every fall, we rise anew,
The journey vast, the skies so blue.

Beyond the hurdles, strength emerges,
With every wave, the spirit surges.
Together we forge, through thick and thin,
In this unbroken race, we begin.

Crown of Intention

Upon the brow, a crown so bright,
Intentions pure, like stars in night.
With open hearts, our paths align,
In every choice, the love will shine.

In gentle acts, the world we mend,
With mindful steps, we learn to bend.
The crown we wear, a sacred trust,
In every moment, it’s love we must.

The Irresistible Pull

In twilight's grasp, the shadows dance,
Hearts drawn close, in a fleeting glance.
With every step, a quiet call,
Entranced, we lean, lest we should fall.

The moon above, a watchful eye,
Guides our way as spirits fly.
A tether strong, we cannot see,
Forever bound, just you and me.

The Pulse of Potential

In the silence, dreams ignite,
Whispers soft, a spark of light.
Every heartbeat, a chance to cease,
Turning doubt into sweet release.

With open arms, the future gleams,
Endless paths, unfurling dreams.
In every moment, hope unfolds,
A tapestry of life retold.

Lanterns in the Mist

Through swirling fog, the lanterns glow,
Casting warmth in the night's flow.
Each flicker tells a story told,
Of journeys new and dreams of old.

Guided by light, we dare to roam,
Finding solace far from home.
In the dance of shadows, we find our way,
Embracing night, welcoming day.

The Garden of Yearning

In a garden where hopes entwine,
Petals whisper, secrets divine.
With every bloom, a heart's request,
To find the peace, to feel the blessed.

Beneath the stars, desires grow,
Yearning deeply, soft and slow.
Each breath a prayer to the night sky,
For love to blossom and never die.

Alight with Conviction

In the dawn's soft glow, we rise,
With fire in our hearts, we aim for the skies.
No fear to hold, no doubt to bide,
Together we march, with courage our guide.

Through shadows deep, we'll carve our way,
Faith lighting paths, come what may.
Each step we take, a promise made,
In the face of storms, we will not fade.

The Road Less Traveled

A winding path through woods so green,
Where few have trod, and few have seen.
With every turn, new sights unfold,
In whispers soft, our dreams are told.

Though thorns may scratch and branches snare,
Each stumble fuels the fire we bear.
Determined hearts and steadfast grace,
On this road, we claim our place.

Whispers of Destiny

In silent nights, when stars align,
The universe speaks, a secret divine.
With hearts attuned to the cosmic song,
We chase the thread where we belong.

For fate's gentle hand guides us still,
Through valleys low and towering hill.
In every choice, a truth to find,
A tapestry woven, our souls intertwined.

Echoes of the Heart

In quiet moments, when shadows loom,
The heart's soft echo fills the room.
With every beat, a story's spun,
Of love and loss, of battles won.

Through laughter's joy and sorrow's tear,
Each whisper carries what we hold dear.
In the depths of silence, we find our way,
Letting echoes guide us, come what may.

Whispers of Destiny

In shadows deep, the secrets lay,
A voice called softly, leading the way.
Stars align, the night's embrace,
We dance with fate, in timeless space.

Echoes linger, tales unfold,
Mysteries wrapped in threads of gold.
With every heartbeat, we draw near,
Whispers of destiny, crystal clear.

Echoes of Purpose

In the silence, a call resonates,
The purpose whispers, it patiently waits.
Each step taken, a song of the heart,
Echoes of purpose, where dreams start.

Count the moments, let them flow,
Through the valley where intentions grow.
In every challenge, a lesson found,
Echoes of purpose, a guiding sound.

The Path Unveiled

Beneath the canopy of ancient trees,
The path unveils with a gentle breeze.
Steps of courage, the journey takes flight,
A tapestry woven by stars at night.

With every fork, choices arise,
Unseen horizons, vast like the skies.
In the heart's compass, truth will prevail,
As we wander the path unveiled.

Threads of Fate

In a loom of time, our stories entwine,
Threads of fate, in patterns divine.
Each twist and turn, a life interweaves,
In the fabric of dreams, the heart believes.

Entangled journeys, we share the light,
Through trials and triumphs, we ignite.
With hearts as one, we navigate space,
Forever united by threads of fate.

Aligning with the Self

In the quiet of dawn's embrace,
Whispers guide the wandering pace.
Each thought a leaf on the stream,
Flowing softly, like a dream.

The heart beats in gentle time,
Rhythm of nature, pure and prime.
Breath by breath, I find my ground,
In stillness, my voice resounds.

Mirrors reflect the truth we seek,
In silence, the spirit speaks.
Forging paths with gentle grace,
Embracing the sacred space.

With every step, I choose to be,
An echo of authenticity.
Aligning my soul with the light,
In unity, I find my sight.

The Compass Within

In the heart, a compass spins,
Guiding me through outs and ins.
With every twist, with every turn,
A light ignites, a flame to burn.

Through forests dense and mountains high,
I seek the truth, I learn to fly.
Each direction whispers clear,
The path unveiled, I have no fear.

Stars align in the velvet night,
As I'm drawn by inner light.
The compass whispers soft and low,
Trust your heart, let your spirit flow.

In shadows deep and valleys wide,
The compass leads, I step with pride.
With every beat, my soul will sing,
A journey forged by what I bring.

Threads of Intention

In the loom of life, threads intertwine,
Each intention a pattern divine.
Weaving dreams with colors bright,
Creating tapestries of light.

With gentle hands, I spin my fate,
Crafting moments, never late.
Every whisper, every choice,
Threads unite to form a voice.

Through joy and sorrow, threads do blend,
A tapestry that knows no end.
In the fibers, stories dwell,
Every heart has tales to tell.

As I tie knots with utmost care,
I find connection everywhere.
Threads of intention, pure and true,
In love's embrace, I start anew.

The Song of the Soul

In the quiet, a melody stirs,
A song that only the heart prefers.
Notes of joy in the gentle breeze,
Harmonies dance between the trees.

From whispers of twilight and dawn,
The soul sings sweetly, never gone.
Each vibration a life reborn,
In every heart, a sacred corn.

With every breath, a note rings true,
Together, we feel the music's hue.
The rhythm flows through every vein,
In perfect sync, we rise again.

So listen closely, friend of light,
The song of the soul sparks the night.
In unity, we find our role,
Together we sing, the song of the soul.

Unwritten Manifesto

In silence, thoughts begin to weave,
A tapestry of dreams we believe.
Words unspoken, a heart's decree,
In shadows, whispers set us free.

With every step, a tale unfolds,
A story written, yet untold.
We gather strength from what's in sight,
A spark ignites amidst the night.

Passions burn within our core,
Together we rise, forever more.
Beneath the weight of stars above,
An unwritten call, a dance of love.

In unity, we find our voice,
In every heartbeat, we rejoice.
An anthem forged in hope's embrace,
Our manifesto, time cannot erase.

Signs in the Twilight

As sun dips low, the colors blend,
A canvas painted, day’s descent.
In fading light, the shadows play,
Whispers of night, beckoning stay.

Stars awaken in velvet skies,
Guiding dreams with ancient ties.
Each twinkle holds a secret song,
A melody where hearts belong.

The moon reflected, soft and bright,
Illumines paths that lead to light.
In twilight’s hush, we find the way,
Connecting dots where spirits sway.

With every heartbeat, signs appear,
In twilight’s grasp, we shed our fear.
Embracing all that dusk bestows,
In fleeting moments, truth still grows.

Journey to the Core

Within the heart, a journey starts,
Through winding paths where shadow parts.
With aim and fire, we seek the light,
A dance of courage in the night.

Beneath the layers, truth resides,
Amidst the chaos, stillness hides.
We peel away the veils of doubt,
Discovering what life’s about.

In silence deep, we hear the call,
A whisper soft that beckons all.
Through trials faced, our spirits soar,
Each step a piece to what’s in store.

With every heartbeat, closer still,
To unearth dreams that spark our will.
The journey winds, yet we must be,
Embracing all that sets us free.

Navigating the Soul's Map

A compass fixed upon the heart,
Guiding souls where dreams impart.
In every twist and turn we take,
A map of moments we create.

Through valleys low, and mountains high,
With open hearts, we learn to fly.
The stars lead us, a cosmic dance,
In fate's embrace, we find our chance.

With every heartbeat, we explore,
The depth of love, forevermore.
In pathways drawn by unseen hands,
We navigate through life's demands.

Each step we take is not in vain,
For every joy is matched with pain.
Yet, on this journey, we will find,
The essence of a life aligned.

In Pursuit of Wholeness

In quiet moments, dreams take flight,
We seek the pieces, lost from sight.
With gentle grace, we mend the fray,
In every heart, a light will stay.

Through tangled paths, we walk as one,
Together shining, brighter sun.
In storms of doubt, we hold our ground,
In unity, our strength is found.

Embers of the Future

Glowing softly in the dark,
The dreams ignite, they leave a mark.
With every spark, a new dawn wakes,
The path ahead expands, and breaks.

We dance with shadows, weave the light,
Embrace the hope that burns so bright.
Each ember whispers of a way,
To guide us forth, come what may.

The Odyssey of Affinity

Two souls entwined on a journey lost,
Through trials faced, we count the cost.
In every laugh, in every tear,
We find the bond that draws us near.

Through distant shores and whispered dreams,
We navigate by love's own themes.
In silences, our hearts will speak,
In every touch, the strong, the weak.

The Soul's Navigation

In darkness deep, the compass glows,
A map of heart, where wisdom flows.
Through valleys low, and peaks of high,
We chart the course, we reach the sky.

With every star, a truth revealed,
In moments still, our fate is sealed.
Through whispers soft, the spirit guides,
In sacred light, the purpose bides.

Drifting Toward Destiny

In the quiet dawn of dreams,
Whispers guide the weary soul,
Stars align in gentle streams,
Fate's embrace makes us whole.

Winds are carrying us near,
Unknown shores bathed in light,
Every heartbeat feels sincere,
As we dance through the night.

Paths converge like rivers flow,
Time's embrace with hands of grace,
With every step, new seeds we sow,
In this vast and timeless space.

Unraveled threads of destiny,
Weaving tales both fierce and bright,
In the tapestry, what will be,
Is written in the stars tonight.

The Path of Embers

Once a flame, now glowing red,
Footsteps mark the scorched ground,
Every spark a word unsaid,
Silent echoes all around.

Through the smoke, a figure stands,
Casting shadows, weaving light,
Guiding hearts with gentle hands,
On the edge of the night.

Memories like ashes drift,
Carried softly on the breeze,
Every moment a precious gift,
Mindful still of memories.

In the darkness, embers gleam,
Illuminating silent fears,
On this path, we find the dream,
Through the laughter and the tears.

Between Hopes and Horizons

Caught between the dusk and dawn,
Promises hang in the air,
Like the light before it's gone,
Fragile dreams call us to dare.

Mountains rise in shadows cast,
Facing storms that test our will,
Every moment fades so fast,
Yet the heart knows to be still.

Oceans wide and skies so clear,
The horizon whispers soft,
Hope unfurls like wings in fear,
Carried gently, we lift off.

In the space where dreams collide,
Life's great journey takes its form,
Between hopes, we choose to bide,
Through the calm and every storm.

Alchemy of the Spirit

In the forge of heart and mind,
Elements blend, merge, and flow,
Transforming what we seek to find,
Into gold, alchemists know.

With each trial, the soul ignites,
Casting doubt into the breeze,
With every struggle, new heights,
Rooted strong like ancient trees.

Lessons learned in heat and fire,
Turning pain to wisdom's gleam,
With each spark, we find our desire,
Chasing ever after the dream.

Through shadows dark and light so bright,
We become what we believe,
In this dance of day and night,
The spirit learns to dream and weave.

The Path Unseen

In shadows cast by ancient trees,
A winding road that bends and weaves.
Through whispers soft of untold dreams,
The heart will guide, or so it seems.

With every step, a tale unfolds,
Of courage found in nights so cold.
The echoes of a past still call,
While destiny awaits us all.

A glimmer shines in faint moonlight,
A chance to chase what feels so right.
With faith as compass, we will go,
The path unseen will help us grow.

In unity with hope we tread,
Embracing journeys yet to spread.
Through forests deep, and skies of blue,
The path unseen awaits anew.

Embrace of Purpose

Awake to find the dawn does break,
With clarity in every ache.
The whispers of the soul's intent,
In every moment's grace is spent.

Through trials faced and battles won,
An ember glows, a radiant sun.
Each heartbeat pulses with belief,
In purpose lies the sweetest relief.

With open arms we can embrace,
The journey mapped, our sacred space.
In every laugh and every tear,
The threads of purpose will be clear.

So forge ahead, let courage swell,
In each endeavor, cast a spell.
With every step, our spirits soar,
Embrace of purpose, evermore.

Beneath the Silent Stars

In velvet skies where silence creeps,
Underneath where starlight sleeps.
A canvas vast, a glow divine,
In cosmic dance, our hearts align.

The night ignites the dreams we chase,
With every twinkle, find our place.
A whispered wish on evening's breeze,
In stillness found, our spirits ease.

The galaxies in their embrace,
Remind us of our humble space.
In unity with all that’s vast,
Beneath the stars, our shadows cast.

So raise your eyes and breathe the night,
In every dark, there lies a light.
Through miles of stardust, hope shall guide,
Beneath the silent stars, we bide.

Journey to the Core

Inward deep, the quest begins,
A journey where the truth spins.
Past layers thick of doubt and fear,
To seek the light that feels so near.

With every twist, a lesson learned,
In silence found, a fire burned.
Resilience blooms in darkest hours,
Awakening to inner powers.

Through tunnels deep, we grasp and hold,
The stories of our hearts unfold.
In every struggle, strength we gain,
A journey rich, a sweet refrain.

Embrace the core, the essence pure,
In self-discovery, we endure.
The journey leads to who we are,
A journey to the core, we spar.

A Map of Inner Fire

Beneath the skin, a flame does flicker,
Shadows dance, a pulse grows quicker.
A compass drawn in dreams so bold,
Guiding paths through stories told.

In quiet nights, the whispers rise,
A symphony of hush and sighs.
Mapping out the heart's desire,
Each point a spark, a fleeting fire.

With every step, the path grows clear,
Embers glow, dissolve the fear.
A journey traced by light and dark,
Igniting hopes, igniting spark.

The inner fire, a force profound,
In every pulse, in every sound.
So may we hold this map in hand,
And walk the line of our own land.

Unraveled Aspirations

Threads of dreams begin to fray,
Woven hopes in disarray.
Each ambition, a tale unfolds,
Revealing truths that time upholds.

Once tightly bound, now loose and wild,
Every heart, a yearning child.
The future calls with open arms,
Yet fear often holds its charms.

In the chaos, find the peace,
From the struggle, let love increase.
Unraveled paths can still align,
In brokenness, the stars still shine.

Let us gather what we've lost,
Reclaim the treasures, count the cost.
With every tear, a lesson learned,
In every heart, the fire burned.

Commitment to the Dream

In the stillness, a promise made,
A spark ignited, won't soon fade.
Through trials faced, we'll persevere,
In every wound, the strength appears.

With passion as our guiding light,
We chase the shadows, banish night.
A dream embraced, we won't let go,
In every heartbeat, let it show.

Commitment carved, like stone so strong,
Together we will right the wrong.
Through storms we rise, through pain we grow,
In every challenge, seeds we sow.

With steadfast hearts, we march in time,
In every rhythm, life’s sweet rhyme.
Fulfilling visions, hand in hand,
Our dreams will flourish, brightly stand.

The Voice of the Unheard

In silence lingers, calls untold,
Voices shiver, dreams unfold.
Echoes dance on barren ground,
In shadows deep, they can be found.

Gather the murmurs, the cries of strife,
Breathe in the whispers, give them life.
For in the quiet lies the truth,
A testament from battered youth.

Lift the veil, let stories soar,
Each untold tale opens a door.
By given voice, the heart expands,
Together we can shift the sands.

Amplify the chords of pain,
In unity, we break the chain.
For every heart that longs to speak,
We rise as one, we grow less weak.

Fragments of the Infinite

In the whispers of the night,
Stars collide in silent dance.
Scattered dreams take fleeting flight,
Fragments lost in cosmic trance.

Time a river, endlessly flows,
Echoes of what might have been.
In each moment, mystery grows,
Life becomes a vivid dream.

Galaxies in silent awe,
Painted skies where wishes gleam.
In our hearts, the universe,
Holds the secrets of our scheme.

From the depths of endless dark,
We rise, seeking the light's embrace.
Every spark ignites a spark,
In the vastness, we find grace.

The Artisan of Fate

With hands of skill, he crafts the day,
Molding dreams into the clay.
Each choice a brushstroke, bold and bright,
Guiding shadows toward the light.

In the silence, whispers grow,
Secrets woven from the flow.
Paths entwined like threads of gold,
Stories waiting to be told.

He spins the wheel of chance and time,
Dancing to a silent rhyme.
Fate an art, both wild and true,
Every moment born anew.

In the heart of every soul,
He finds the pieces to behold.
An artisan with endless grace,
In each life, he leaves his trace.

Pillars of Passion

In the heart of flame, we rise,
Pillars strong against the skies.
With courage forged in endless night,
We defend our dreams with might.

Each heartbeat echoes, pure and loud,
A testament, we stand proud.
In our fervor, we ignite,
A wildfire, blazing through the night.

Voices join, a vibrant song,
In unity, we all belong.
Chasing visions, bold and free,
Together, we create our spree.

Through trials faced and battles fought,
In the fire, we've been taught.
Passion fuels our every stride,
As we journey side by side.

A Symphony of Self

In the quiet, self unfolds,
A melody that takes its hold.
Notes of laughter, whispers deep,
In the stillness, secrets seep.

Each heartbeat sings a story rare,
A tapestry woven with care.
With every step, a rhythm found,
In the essence, we are bound.

Chords of joy and strains of sorrow,
Create the hopes of a bright tomorrow.
In the harmony of life's embrace,
We dance to the time and space.

A symphony, ever evolving,
In the chaos, love resolving.
With every rise and every fall,
We find the music in us all.

Casting the Anchor

In the harbor, tides pull and sway,
The boat alone must find its way.
Casting the anchor with hopeful might,
A calm heart braces for the night.

Fading sun on the water's skin,
Whispers of waves where dreams begin.
With every toss, a wish set free,
Anchored deep in the heart's sea.

Stars appear, a guiding light,
Through silent depths, in shadowed flight.
Tethering hopes to the endless blue,
Night's embrace offers dreams anew.

Morning blooms on horizon's face,
Release the anchor, find your place.
A journey starts with every thread,
Sailing forth where the heart is led.

Roots of Reverie

Underneath the ancient trees,
Roots entwined with whispered breeze.
Dreams are buried deep within,
Sprouting hope where life begins.

Branches reach to the sky so wide,
In their shade, our secrets hide.
Echoes of laughter and soft delight,
Nurtured by love through darkest night.

In the soil, memories gleam,
Cultivating a world of dreams.
The heart takes root beneath the ground,
In stillness, our purpose is found.

Seasons shift, yet we remain,
Bound together through joy and pain.
From roots of reverie, we ascend,
Growing stronger as we transcend.

The Invisible Guiding Hand

In silence, a touch we cannot see,
Guiding lives like leaves from a tree.
Whispers of fate through tangled threads,
In every step, the heart is led.

Through shadows deep and valleys wide,
A gentle force walks by our side.
Unseen currents shape our way,
Leading us into light of day.

In moments lost, when hope feels thin,
A hand appears where we begin.
With every stumble, every fall,
A tender push, we rise through all.

As paths unfold and destinies bend,
Trust the journey, let love amend.
For in the silence, we will find,
The invisible guiding hand, so kind.

Constellations of Conviction

Beneath the night, the stars ignite,
Painting dreams in silvery light.
Constellations dance in the cosmic sea,
Illuminating what's meant to be.

Each twinkle speaks in ancient tongue,
Stories of battles lost and won.
In the depths, aspirations rise,
Guided by the truth in our skies.

Horizons stretch, horizons bend,
Through every journey, our spirits mend.
In shadows cast, we find our way,
Listening close to what stars say.

With every heartbeat, every sigh,
We gather strength, let spirits fly.
Underneath these constellations grand,
We hold the light with steadfast hand.

Beneath the Surface of Dreams

In the stillness of the night,
Whispers dance like stars above,
Where shadows weave their tales of light,
And hopes awaken, filled with love.

Beneath the dreams, the currents flow,
A tapestry of hidden fears,
Yet in the heart, the ember's glow,
Ignites the path through veils of tears.

Adrift in realms of soft embrace,
Each thought a ripple, gently cast,
In the depths, we seek a place,
Where future echoes of the past.

So dive beneath the surface bright,
Embrace the waves with open arms,
For in the depths, there lies the light,
A treasure trove of timeless charms.

Chasing Tomorrow's Light

Beneath the dawn, a promise stirs,
A golden path where dreams take flight,
We follow hope on gentle whirs,
In pursuit of tomorrow’s light.

Through tangled trails and hidden ways,
With every step, our spirits soar,
In the embrace of sunlit rays,
We find the strength to want much more.

Each heartbeat echoes like a drum,
A symphony of life's sweet call,
As shadows fade and we become,
The warriors who defy the fall.

With open hearts, we chart our course,
Through storms and calm, the journey's art,
Chasing the dreams with fierce discourse,
And lighting up the darkest heart.

Heartstrings and Horizons

Across the skies, the colors blend,
Where heartstrings pull with tender grace,
In the horizon, dreams descend,
And take their shape in boundless space.

With every note, our spirits swell,
A symphony of hopes and fears,
In melodies, the stories tell,
Of laughter shared and quiet tears.

The compass spins with every breath,
A guide through realms both near and far,
In every heartbeat lies the quest,
To find the light in every star.

So let us dance upon the waves,
With open hearts, our lives entwined,
For in the journey, love can save,
The compass points to what's designed.

The Compass Within

In silent moments, truth reveals,
The compass that we hold inside,
Through veils of doubt, our spirit heals,
Guiding us like a gentle tide.

Each flicker sparks the inner flame,
A beacon through the darkest night,
With every challenge, we proclaim,
The strength to rise and seek the light.

Through winding paths, we roam and sway,
The heart, a map of every choice,
With courage as our true ballet,
We dance to life's unending voice.

So trust the compass, feel its pull,
For deep within, our dreams await,
With every heartbeat, ever full,
We chart the course, we navigate.

The Vessel of the Vision

In the quiet of night, dreams take flight,
Carried by whispers, under starlight.
A vessel of hopes, so fragile yet strong,
Sailing through shadows, where we belong.

With each passing wave, the past begins to fade,
A tapestry woven, where memories are laid.
Guided by the compass of our heart's desire,
Illuminated paths, set the spirit on fire.

Through currents of doubt, we'll find our way,
Navigating storms, come what may.
In the heart of the vessel, a beacon shines bright,
Holding our visions, deep in the night.

Together we journey, through silence and sound,
In the vessel of vision, our souls are unbound.
With courage and grace, we rise from the deep,
Awakening dreams, as the universe sleeps.

Heartbeats of Tomorrow

Every heartbeat, a rhythm of time,
Echoing softly like a distant chime.
In the stillness, we find the spark,
A promise of dawn, dispelling the dark.

With every breath, the future unfolds,
Painting our story in colors so bold.
Dreams intertwine in a delicate dance,
As fate gives us space, we take our chance.

Together we build on the hopes we've sown,
In the garden of time, seeds of love are grown.
With hearts wide open, we welcome the light,
Embracing the warmth that ignites the night.

In heartbeats of tomorrow, we find our way,
Guided by whispers that never decay.
As the world spins, we stand side by side,
With courage to face whatever may bide.

Waves of Inspiration

Crashing tides rush with stories untold,
In the whispers of waves, we find jewels of gold.
Each crest a muse, each fall a release,
In the dance of the ocean, we discover peace.

From the depths of the blue, inspiration flows,
In the vastness of life, creativity grows.
As the sea calls to those who dare dream,
We ride the waves of a shimmering gleam.

With colors of sunset spilling the shore,
The art of existence reveals evermore.
In the rhythm of water, our spirits align,
Crafting visions that inevitably shine.

For every wave holds a spark of the divine,
Inspiring the heart with a sacred design.
As we surf through the moments, lost and found,
The waves of inspiration, forever surround.

When Dreams Awaken

In the stillness, the dawn breaks renewed,
When dreams awaken, hopes are imbued.
Soft rays of sunlight kiss slumbering eyes,
Opening the door to limitless skies.

From whispers of night, we rise with intent,
Casting aside all doubts that once bent.
With courage ignited, we step into light,
Embracing the magic that blooms in our sight.

Through valleys of struggle and mountains of grace,
We chase after visions with purest embrace.
In the moment of reckoning, we find our way,
As dreams come alive in the brightness of day.

When dreams awaken, we're destined to fly,
Finding our wings and learning to try.
In the journey of life, we craft our own art,
When dreams awaken, we follow the heart.

The Art of Being

In silence, wisdom flows like streams,
A dance of thoughts, in quiet dreams.
With every breath, life takes its form,
Embracing now, in softest warm.

The heart beats slow, with steady grace,
In every moment, we find our place.
The art of being, simple, clear,
In present time, we draw near.

With open eyes, the world unfolds,
A tapestry of stories told.
Each fleeting joy, a treasure found,
In stillness deep, our souls are bound.

Together here, we share the light,
Our spirits soar, like birds in flight.
In every breath, a chance to see,
The beauty of this mystery.

Labyrinth of Longing

In shadows deep, the heart does roam,
Through twisting paths, it seeks a home.
Each turn reveals a glimpse of fate,
A whispered wish, the hands of fate.

Across the maze, the echoes call,
The yearning souls, they rise, they fall.
With every step, a hope ignites,
A flickering flame in endless nights.

Yet in the dark, a strength is born,
From tangled roots, we rise each morn.
Though lost at times, we will persist,
Through winding ways, we find our tryst.

So walk with me, through night and day,
In this labyrinth, we'll find our way.
With hearts as guides, we'll light the path,
In searching souls, there lies our wrath.

Horizon of Hope

The dawn breaks soft with golden rays,
A promise whispered in morning haze.
With every step towards the light,
We chase our dreams, we lift our sight.

Beyond the hills, the sky expands,
A canvas vast, in unseen hands.
Each color born from challenges faced,
In shades of courage, hope embraced.

With open hearts, we brave the storms,
Through trials deep, our spirit warms.
In unity, we rise and stand,
As one, we draw a brighter land.

So let us reach beyond the veil,
Where whispers of tomorrow sail.
A horizon wide, where futures glow,
In every heart, the seeds we sow.

A Journey without Borders

With every step, we travel wide,
Through open fields, the world our guide.
No fences built to hold us back,
In boundless skies, we find our track.

From mountains high to rivers deep,
In nature's embrace, our dreams we keep.
Each path we tread, a story unfolds,
In whispered tales, our spirit molds.

In foreign lands, we find our kin,
With shared laughter, the ties begin.
No walls between, just hearts that share,
A journey rich, beyond compare.

So wander free, with arms out wide,
Let love be our eternal guide.
In every corner, friendship grows,
With open hearts, the world bestows.

Moments of Clarity

In silence, thoughts align,
Truth emerges, a spark divine.
The chaos fades, a gentle breeze,
A whisper of calm among the trees.

Eyes open wide to the dawn of grace,
Each heartbeat, a step in a sacred space.
In fleeting seconds, the world stands still,
Moments of clarity, a soul to fulfill.

The past recedes, shadows grow light,
Hope blossoms like flowers bright.
In the clarity, love finds its way,
Guiding the heart to the light of day.

Embrace the now, let worries take flight,
In moments of clarity, the spirit takes flight.
With open hearts, we journey afar,
Finding ourselves in the light of a star.

Footprints on Untrodden Paths

Each step unfolds a new embrace,
A journey begun, with dreams to chase.
Footprints left on soil untouched,
Whispers of courage, a heart uncrutched.

Through woods of wonder, we roam and weave,
In the tapestry of life, we believe.
The horizon calls with a voice so clear,
Footprints on paths where none draw near.

Moments of doubt, like shadows creep,
Yet in the journey, we find our leap.
With every step, we learn to see,
The beauty of paths that set us free.

Together we wander, hand in hand,
On untrodden paths across the land.
With every footprint, a story unfolds,
In the book of life, our spirit bold.

Illuminated Longings

Under the stars, dreams take flight,
Illuminated longings, glowing bright.
Hearts whisper softly to the night,
Desires unfurl, souls igniting light.

In the quietude, love softly sighs,
Echoes of wishes in the skies.
Each longing a thread woven anew,
Illuminated whispers guiding us through.

Flickers of hope dance in the dark,
Illuminated longings ignite a spark.
On the canvas of night, we paint with care,
Our dreams unfurling, as we lay them bare.

In the silence, the heart finds its song,
With illuminated longings, we belong.
Together we wander, fate intertwined,
In the glow of our dreams, our essence aligned.

The Symphony of Self-Discovery

Each note we play in life's grand score,
A symphony waiting to explore.
Through highs and lows, melodies rise,
In the dance of moments, our spirit flies.

In echoes of laughter, tears unfold,
The symphony whispers secrets untold.
With every heartbeat, we find our tune,
Self-discovery beneath the moon.

Chords of love and strings of grace,
The rhythm of life, a warm embrace.
In melodies soft, our souls align,
The symphony beckons, divine design.

Together we harmonize, dreams unfurled,
In this beautiful symphony, our hearts are whirled.
With every step, we compose our song,
In the symphony of self, we all belong.

The Call of the Wild

In the forest, whispers roam,
Beneath the ancient trees, they call.
The wind's embrace, a soothing balm,
Nature’s voice, a beckoning thrall.

Mountains rise to touch the sky,
Rivers dance, relentless flow.
Echoes of the wild invite,
To venture forth where few dare go.

Stars alight as night descends,
Creatures stir in shadowed grace.
The wild is where the heart transcends,
In freedom’s arms, we find our place.

Adventure waits in every glade,
In every step, new stories bloom.
Together with the earth, unafraid,
We answer nature’s endless room.

Whispers in the Fog

Morning mist wraps the world tight,
Soft secrets held in silken shrouds.
Voices linger, lost from sight,
As shadows dance with ghostly crowds.

Paths concealed in hazy dreams,
Mysteries linger where clouds curl.
In the stillness, silence screams,
The fog weaves tales yet to unfurl.

Footsteps echo on the dew,
Every step a chance to hear.
The whispers call, both old and new,
Drawing hearts to what is dear.

As the sun breaks through the gray,
Secrets fade in light's warm grasp.
Yet the echoes won't drift away,
In fog, the heart learns to clasp.

Pathways of the Heart

In every choice, a path unfolds,
Winding through the soul's embrace.
Love's compass points, both brave and bold,
Guides us toward our destined place.

Steps taken softly, in the light,
With whispers of dreams we chase.
In shadows deep, we seek the bright,
For hope ignites in love's warm space.

Through valleys low and mountains high,
Every turn a step to dare.
With courage found, we learn to fly,
To follow truths, we freely share.

And when the road seems far and long,
In hearts united, we belong.
For every pathway, whether right or wrong,
Leads us deeper into love's strong song.

The Canvas of Ambition

A blank expanse, the canvas lies,
Waiting for dreams to take their flight.
With strokes of passion, bold and wise,
We paint our goals in colors bright.

Ambition flows like rivers deep,
In every hue, our visions gleam.
With every challenge, we shall leap,
To mold our future from a dream.

Brush in hand, we carve our fate,
With every dab, a vision born.
Though trials tempt us to create,
In faith, we rise with every dawn.

As layers build, the story grows,
In mastery, we find our start.
Each color tells what courage shows,
The canvas reflects the beating heart.

Fragrance of the Unlived

In dreams we wander, paths untold,
Moments linger, life unfolds.
Whispers of joy, shadows of pain,
The scent of hope, in each refrain.

Memories forgotten, yet still they glow,
Dancing in twilight, softly they flow.
Fragrant wildflowers, blooming unseen,
A tapestry woven, where we might have been.

The heart remembers, even when lost,
Embracing the echoes, no matter the cost.
In silence they linger, these untrodden ways,
The fragrance of dreams haunts mundane days.

So cherish the whispers of what could have been,
In the garden of dreams, let the journey begin.
Each petal a promise, a beautiful sigh,
Fragrance of the unlived, it never will die.

Shadows of the Old Road

Beneath the trees where secrets lie,
Echoes of laughter blend with the sigh.
Time has a way of fading the light,
Shadows grow longer, as day turns to night.

Cobblestones whisper of journeys past,
Footsteps of travelers, shadows they cast.
The stories they carry, etched in the stone,
In silence they linger, never alone.

Old lanterns flicker, guiding the way,
Through darkened paths where shadows play.
Memories linger, in the cool, crisp air,
The old road beckons, if you dare.

In the twilight hour, dreams intertwine,
Lost in the shadows, the heart will align.
Each step we take, a reverie found,
On shadows of the old road, wisdom abounds.

Rising from Within

When the dawn breaks, a soft embrace,
The light awakens, ignites the space.
Wings of the spirit begin to spread,
Hope takes flight, where fear once tread.

Whispers of courage, gentle and clear,
Rise from the ashes, silencing fear.
In every heartbeat, the flame is stoked,
Through trials faced, strength evokes.

A garden of dreams, nurtured in time,
Each challenge faced, a reason to climb.
Beneath the surface, potential alive,
From the depths of the soul, we strive to thrive.

So let the sun shine, let shadows fade,
Unlock the power, in silence laid.
Rising from within, our spirit will soar,
Embracing the light, forever more.

Threads of Destiny

In the loom of life, we weave our fate,
Threads intertwining, both delicate and great.
Colors of joy, and shades of despair,
A tapestry woven with love and care.

Every chance taken, a stitch in the seam,
Paths that diverge, and yet always dream.
Through trials and tribulations, we find our way,
Threads of destiny guide us, come what may.

With every heartbeat, a pattern unfolds,
Stories of courage in silken threads told.
Fate's gentle hand, weaving designs,
In the fabric of time, the universe aligns.

So cherish each thread, in life's grand design,
For through every moment, the stars align.
Threads of destiny, forever entwined,
In the fabric of life, our souls are defined.

Awakening the Dreamer

In quiet night, whispers call,
Softly beckoning, dreamers all.
Stars alight with tales untold,
Awake the hearts, let dreams unfold.

In fields of hope, we take our flight,
Chasing visions, banishing night.
With every breath, we claim our space,
Awakening truths we now embrace.

Together we dance, in the moon's glow,
With every step, the wild winds blow.
Embracing change, we rise and soar,
Awakening the dreamer at our core.

In this moment, we find our way,
Reclaiming joy, come what may.
Lighting our path, we boldly go,
Awakening the dreamer, let love flow.

The Light Within Shadows

Amidst the dark, a flicker gleams,
Illuminating hidden dreams.
In shadows deep, a soul ignites,
Finding strength in the quiet nights.

With every doubt, the heart will shine,
Casting aside what’s dark, malign.
For in the depths where silence sings,
The light within, true courage brings.

Beneath the veil, the truth will grow,
A dance with fears, a gentle flow.
Embracing light, through trials faced,
Transforming shadows, love embraced.

Together we rise, hand in hand,
Nurtured by hope, we take a stand.
In the storm's eye, we find our peace,
The light within shadows shall never cease.

Chasing the Radiant Horizon

Upon the dawn, new colors spread,
With every step, our hearts are fed.
Chasing dreams on wings of grace,
Finding joy in every place.

The horizon calls, a vibrant song,
In its embrace, we feel we belong.
With open arms, we greet the day,
Chasing the radiant light's ballet.

Through valleys low and mountains high,
We search for truth beneath the sky.
Connected still, in every breath,
Chasing horizons, conquering death.

With every sunrise, hope renews,
A canvas wide, painted with hues.
Chasing the dreams that lift us near,
To the radiant horizon, crystal clear.

Dance of Authenticity

In the rhythm of our hearts, we sway,
With every beat, we find our way.
Authentic dreams, like petals spread,
In the dance of life, we forge ahead.

Through laughter bright and sorrows deep,
We honor all, the promise we keep.
In the mirror's gaze, we find our truth,
The dance of authenticity, eternal youth.

United in passion, we move as one,
With open spirits, fear comes undone.
In every twirl, a story's told,
Of courage found and hearts made bold.

So let us dance beneath the stars,
Embracing all, forgetting scars.
In every step, our essence shines,
The dance of authenticity, where love aligns.

Seeds of Authenticity

In the soil of our being, they lie,
Dreams waiting to bloom under the sky.
Tending to them with love every day,
They whisper the truths we long to say.

Nurtured in silence, they quietly grow,
With roots intertwined, they flourish and glow.
Fears fade away as courage ignites,
Seeds of authenticity reach for the heights.

With every step taken, our essence is found,
In the dance of our souls, we break from the ground.
Lifting the veil of what's false and inane,
We cultivate gardens, blossoming in pain.

Authentic voices ringing true and clear,
Embracing the shadows, we banish the fear.
As we share our stories, unveiled and free,
The seeds once dormant now flourish to be.

Harmonies of the Heart

In gentle whispers, the heart speaks low,
Melodies crafted in the ebb and flow.
Each beat a note in a song divine,
Binding our spirits, your heart and mine.

Through trials faced, and sorrows shared,
In symphonic echoes, we've always cared.
Rhythms emerging from moments of grace,
Creating a chorus in time and space.

With every kindness, a harmony swells,
Uniting our stories, like magical spells.
Hands held together, we walk this path,
Finding sweet solace in love's warm bath.

The crescendo rises, breaking the night,
As hearts intertwine under soft silver light.
A symphony crafted with notes pure and right,
Together we sing till the dawn is in sight.

The Alchemy of Aspirations

In the furnace of hope, dreams turn to gold,
Transforming desires, brave souls unrolled.
Elements mingling in passionate dance,
Brewing potentials, igniting a chance.

With visions ablaze like stars in the dark,
Crafting our futures, we ignite the spark.
Elixirs of courage in every breath drawn,
Alchemy blooms with the rise of the dawn.

In each sacred moment, intentions align,
Shaping our journeys, through valleys we climb.
A tapestry woven from threads of our will,
In the heat of our yearning, we find our thrill.

Through trials and triumphs, we gather our might,
Chasing horizons and dreams taking flight.
The alchemy whispers, “Your heart is the key,”
Unlocking the worlds that are waiting to be.

Unfolding the Hidden Self

With layers of mystery wrapped tight in our skin,
We peel back the shadows, where love can begin.
Each revelation, a puzzle unturned,
In the light of our truth, the soul's flame has burned.

Like petals unfurling, in soft morning light,
We discover the beauty concealed from our sight.
Fragments of courage, we gather and blend,
Healing the wounds as the darkness can mend.

In the dance of unveiling, we find who we are,
An odyssey painted with each shining star.
With hearts open wide, we embrace the unknown,
In the garden of self, we've finally grown.

Through courage and patience, we gently explore,
The depths of our being, revealing much more.
Unfolding the layers, we learn to believe,
In the power of self, and the love we can weave.

Constellations of Meaning

In the night sky, dreams take flight,
Whispered secrets in the starlight.
Patterns form in dark expanse,
Guiding hearts to take a chance.

Each star shines with stories untold,
Lessons of love, brave and bold.
Connections drawn from light years past,
In this universe, shadows cast.

We seek our truth in cosmic dance,
Finding hope in every glance.
Galaxies spin, weaving fate,
In the vastness, we contemplate.

With every spark, we find our way,
Learning from night, embracing day.
Constellations guide our sea,
Navigating what's meant to be.

The Courage to Become

Stepping forth into the light,
Facing fears that take their flight.
Breaking chains that held us tight,
With each breath, we spark our might.

Dreams awaken from their sleep,
Daring souls no longer weep.
In the shadows, strength ignites,
With each challenge, spirit heights.

Rising from the depths we fall,
Listening to our inner call.
Embracing cracks that let us grow,
In vulnerability, we glow.

With courage woven in our seams,
We transform our silent dreams.
Through struggles, we find our own,
In becoming, we are shown.

Beyond the Masks We Wear

Masks of laughter, masks of pain,
Hiding truths, our hearts in chain.
Behind the smiles, shadows creep,
In silence, secrets we keep.

Yearning to shed these fragile guises,
Discovering strength that surprises.
Layers peeled, the soul laid bare,
Finding solace in the air.

With every breath, the masks start to fade,
Embracing selves we once betrayed.
A journey deep to know our core,
Revealing love forevermore.

In unity with every scar,
We dance beneath a distant star.
Beyond the masks, we learn to see,
The beauty of simply being free.

In Pursuit of Inner Truth

Quiet whispers in the night,
Seeking wisdom, chasing light.
Within the stillness, hearts align,
In pursuit of the divine.

Questions echo, softly posed,
Unraveling what we've enclosed.
Every layer, one step deep,
In this journey, secrets keep.

Flames of doubt may flicker bright,
Yet we turn to face the fight.
Truth unfolds in gentle ways,
Guiding us through winding maze.

Trust the shadows, trust the pain,
In their depths, we break the chain.
In pursuit of what is real,
We embrace all that we feel.

Stellar Reflections

In the night sky, stars will gleam,
Whispers of light, a cosmic dream.
Guiding souls through the vast unknown,
Each twinkle tells of journeys flown.

Moonlight dances on a tranquil sea,
Echoes of worlds, wild and free.
Constellations mark our sacred path,
Reminders of fate, love, and wrath.

Galaxies swirl in a twinkling wave,
Silent stories of those who brave.
Through the cosmos, hearts ignite,
Stellar reflections, pure and bright.

Celestial wonders call to the heart,
Binding us close, never apart.
In the vast vacuum, we find our way,
Lost in the night, yet found in the day.

The Language of the Soul

Words unspoken, whispers of grace,
Echoes of feelings that time can't erase.
In the silence, truths arise,
The language of the soul never lies.

Glimmers of passion in a glance,
Subtle cues in a fleeting dance.
Heartbeats relay the tales untold,
In every moment, warmth unfolds.

Laughter and tears blend like dreams,
Expressions flow like gentle streams.
In every sigh, the essence sings,
The language of love that eternity brings.

Connected we are, thread by thread,
In the tapestry of life, we're led.
To understand, to touch, to feel,
The language of the soul is real.

The Essence of Belonging

In the hearts of friends, warmth does glow,
A gathering place where love can flow.
Every laugh shared, a bond that grows,
The essence of belonging knows no throes.

Embraced by kindness, surrounded by care,
A refuge found in laughter we share.
With every story, connections ignite,
In the fabric of trust, we find our light.

In moments of strife, we rise as one,
Joined together, we've already won.
Through the seasons, in joy or pain,
The essence of belonging will ever remain.

Together we stand, hand in hand,
In the comfort of love, we'll always stand.
Through the storm, we carry along,
In the essence of belonging, we grow strong.

Roots of a Dream

Deep in the ground, where wishes reside,
Roots entwined, they reach far and wide.
Nurtured by hope and the sun's warm rays,
Germinating visions that time delays.

In the quiet earth, ambitions take hold,
Whispers of promise, stories untold.
The strength of our roots pushes us high,
Chasing the clouds, where the eagles fly.

Through trials and storms, we bend but don't break,
Grounded in dreams, we choose to partake.
In the struggle, we find our true worth,
The roots of a dream give life to the earth.

With every dawn, new beginnings arise,
Awakening hopes under vast open skies.
Bound to our journey, we strive to believe,
In the roots of a dream, we dare to achieve.

The Pulse of Promise

In whispers soft, the future calls,
A heart that beats, through rise and falls.
Each hope ignites, a spark anew,
A journey waits, for me and you.

In shadows cast, we find our way,
Through darkest nights, to brightest day.
With every step, the path unwinds,
In every breath, the strength we find.

The seeds of dreams, in soil they lie,
With time they grow, to touch the sky.
A promise made, in trust we stand,
Together bound, hand in hand.

The Firefly's Flight

In twilight's glow, a dance begins,
With fading light, where time still spins.
A flicker bright, through evening's veil,
A gentle spark, on breezes sail.

Amongst the reeds, they weave and dart,
A fleeting glimpse, ignites the heart.
With every pulse, they share their song,
In unity, where we belong.

Their glowing trails, like dreams in flight,
Illuminate the depths of night.
In moments shared, in laughter's light,
A firefly's flight, pure and bright.

Wings of Remembrance

In faded hues, the past takes wing,
Soft echoes of what memories bring.
Each gentle breeze, a tale retold,
In whispers shared, the heart's pure gold.

The skies adorned with stories high,
Of love once lost, and dreams that fly.
With every beat, the heart recalls,
The moments held, behind these walls.

Through time we soar, on wings of light,
In shadows cast, in dreams so bright.
The tales we weave, in silence kept,
Are wings of heart, where memories slept.

Pebbles in the Stream

In waters clear, the pebbles rest,
Each one a tale, a treasure blessed.
The currents flow, with gentle grace,
Time whispers soft, in this sacred space.

Each ripple forms, a dance of days,
In sunlight's glow, where nature plays.
Smooth stones reflect, the joy of ease,
In nature's arms, the heart finds peace.

Along the banks, the wildflowers bloom,
Their colors bright, dispel the gloom.
In every glance, the stream unfolds,
The stories etched, as life beholds.

Embracing the Unseen

In shadows deep, we find our way,
Where whispers softly guide the strays.
With every step, the heart takes flight,
Embracing dreams hidden from sight.

The moonlit path unveils the truth,
A dance of hope, eternal youth.
Beyond the veil, the magic glows,
Unseen wonders, our souls compose.

Beneath the stars, we cast our fears,
Painting light with laughter and tears.
In silence, faith begins to rise,
Embracing worlds beyond the skies.

So let the unseen cradle our hearts,
For every end is where hope starts.
With open arms and trusting minds,
We'll cherish all the love that binds.

Dancing with Possibility

In every heartbeat, rhythms call,
We sway together, never fall.
With open hands, we seize the air,
Dancing with dreams, beyond despair.

Each twirl a chance, each leap a sky,
Embracing joy as moments fly.
Across the floor, the future shines,
In every glance, a world aligns.

We close our eyes to feel the light,
In every breath, we take to flight.
With hope our guide, we will not cease,
Dancing with possibility, we find peace.

So let the music carry on,
Through open fields, till the dawn.
We'll chase the stars, let spirits blend,
Dancing with life, around each bend.

Resonance of the Inner Voice

A whisper stirs within the soul,
Echoes of truth, they make us whole.
In quiet moments, we must listen,
For every doubt, a spark's ignition.

With gentle tones, it softly cries,
A melody that never lies.
In each heartbeat, wisdom flows,
Resonance that only the heart knows.

Through stormy skies and gentle rains,
The inner voice, it breaks our chains.
In tender thoughts, we find our path,
Guided by love, we feel its wrath.

So trust the sound that leads you home,
In sacred echoes, we shall roam.
For every fear, let courage rise,
Resonance blooms beneath the skies.

Shifting Sands of Ambition

Amidst the dunes, our dreams emerge,
With every grain, our hearts converge.
The winds of change, they sweep and spin,
Shifting sands where strength begins.

With every step, the future calls,
Through highs and lows, we face the fall.
In daring leaps, we chase the sun,
Shifting sands, our race begun.

Navigating tides and winds anew,
Each vision born, a promise true.
With grit and grace, we carve our name,
In shifting sands, we play the game.

So let us rise, despite the fears,
Transform the doubts, dry every tear.
In every grain, our hopes expand,
Navigating life, shifting sands.

Printed in the USA
CPSIA information can be obtained
at www.ICGtesting.com
LVHW050351151024
793846LV00001B/253

9 789916 880371